MANGA TO THE MAX

Drawing and Coloring Book

WARRIORS

ART AND STORY BY

Erik DePrince

WRITTEN BY

Erik DePrince and Jess Volinski

DESIGN ORIGINALS

an Imprint of Fox Chapel Publishing

www.d-originals.com

HISTORY OF THE UNITED EARTH ENFORCEMENT (UEE)

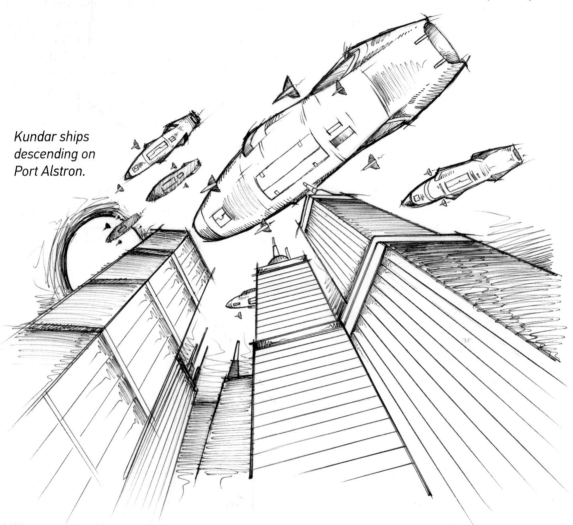

Kundar ships descending on Port Alstron.

Earth was not always the protected planet it is today, defended by artificially intelligent robots, Dragon Guardians, and warriors. Before the alien Incoming, before the Corporate Consolidation, and before the Kundar attack at Port Alstron, the 2100s were a time of great vulnerability and tragedy on Earth.

Between the years 2090 and 2140, the effects of overpopulation and climate change hit a tipping point. Tropical areas became so hot they were uninhabitable, rising oceans flooded coastal cities, vicious storms ripped across the planet, crops failed and famine reigned, and governments collapsed. Humanity faced each of these hardships and adapted. We used our technological advances to solve as many problems as possible. Out of desperation came innovation.

But in 2142, three catastrophic earthquakes occurred in a single month, triggering worldwide tsunamis and volcanic eruptions. Tragedy shook every corner of the globe and brought the planet to the brink of collapse. In the next twenty years, almost 10 billion people on Earth died, most of starvation and disease. At the planet's peak population in 2089, there were 18 billion people worldwide. By 2175, there were only 1 billion. It was humanity's darkest period.

But then the Earth began to heal. Some said it was because of the decreased population; others claimed that large corporations were working together secretly to deploy weather-altering technology. Whatever the cause, things began to get better. Violent weather lessened and natural disasters became rarer. Hot temperatures dropped and crop yields increased. By 2192, life was improving around the world. Thousands of corporations merged and reorganized in what history would call the Great Consolidation. In the end, five corporations emerged, each one ruling one of the five zones of Earth.

By the time we had our first contact with alien life in 2216, when delegates from the United Empires (UE) arrived on Earth, the planet had faced extreme adversity and triumphed. So when the UE made an offer for us to join them, we declined. We had proved to ourselves that we could solve our own problems and didn't need to be part of some far-off Empire. The UE accepted our

With an assembled fighting force of ten million humans and incomers fighting side by side with thousands of Artillery Siege Mechs, Earth's forces descended on the port and took it back in a terrible battle, fighting off the Kundar until they retreated. The fight lasted 11 days and resulted in more than seven million human and incomer casualties. But the horrible event united the world. Everyone realized it was time to come together to create an organized planetary defense.

In 2228, the world's ruling corporations merged in the ultimate consolidation to create the United Earth Enforcement (UEE), becoming the protectors of the planet. Combining our technology with alien technology

This horrible event united the world. Everyone realized it was time to come together to create an organized planetary defense.

decision and left peacefully. But now Earth was on the map, and everyone in the Empires knew we were here. With our doors thrown open, many beings from other worlds came to Earth looking for a better life and new opportunities; the Incoming had begun.

After humanity's population losses, we had plenty of room on the planet, so we welcomed as many incomers as possible. These new inhabitants brought with them technology and information, now Earth's two most prized resources. Alien technology helped us to discover new ways to continue the planet's healing process. But along with the benefits that incomers brought came an equal number of challenges, including a steady rise in crime from the influx of criminals eager to operate outside of the UE's reach.

For three years, incomers peacefully entered the planet through the intergalactic Alstron Space Port without incident. But that peace was shortlived; in 2227 there was an attack on the port from a power-hungry fringe world of the UE called the Kundar Empire. Several thousand Kundar struck Alstron Space Port with an assault fleet of battle cruisers and an entire battalion of Kundar Artillery, capturing the port within twenty-four hours.

The corporations of Earth scrambled to work together to face this threat; the alternative was clearly the extinction of the human race. On the day of the invasion, the corporations of the world united and mounted a siege, putting aside differences to pool their resources.

brought by the incomers, the UEE developed many robots and cybernetic AI to police and protect the planet. The UEE also recruited and trained a diverse range of warriors.

More help was also on the way, taking an unexpected form. Teirin was the first of many dragons to arrive on earth in 2234, seeking safe haven and the opportunity to heal after millennia of being hunted for sport by the Empires. In exchange for cybernetic upgrades from the UEE, these dragons promised to protect the planet and became known as the Dragon Guardians, adding great might to our defenses.

The arrival of Dragons encouraged another warrior class to emerge on Earth, a group who had remained hidden for hundreds of years out of fear of persecution. Brilliant, powerful, and seemingly immortal, Dragon Walkers have the body of a human, the soul of a dragon, and powerful psychic and physical abilities. Dragon Walkers experienced an increase in their abilities once Teirin arrived, and their powers grow with each new dragon that comes to Earth.

It is now 2238. Earth has changed dramatically in response to learning that we are not alone in the universe, and those changes have made us stronger, more unified, and more diverse than ever. With the planet now protected by robots, Dragon Guardians, and warriors, we are ready to respond to any threat, prepared for whatever is coming next.

7 STEPS TO CRAFTING A CHARACTER

1. Planning

2. Creating a Framework

3. Blocking in Shapes

4. Defining Forms

5. Refining Forms

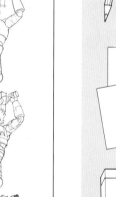

6. Inking the Final Lines

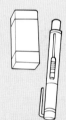

7. Adding Color
  • Light Source and Shading
  • Blocking in Color
  • Gradients
  • Shadows
  • Highlights

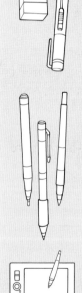

In this drawing and coloring lesson, I'm going to guide you through my process of crafting an original character, from initial notes to final colored art, in 7 basic steps.

DRAWING MATERIALS YOU'LL NEED

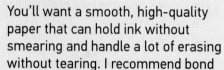

• **PENCILS:**
Any pencil you're comfortable with will work, but I recommend mechanical pencils with .5 mm lead in either H or HB hardness.

• **PAPER:**
You'll want a smooth, high-quality paper that can hold ink without smearing and handle a lot of erasing without tearing. I recommend bond paper, bleedproof paper, or a thick, high-quality copy paper.

• **ERASERS:**
Have a variety on hard, and don't be afraid to use them! I especially like the thin retractable kind to get into smaller areas.

• **PENS:**
Everyone has favorite pens, so I recommend you use what you're most comfortable with. Have a variety of tip sizes on hand so you can vary the thickness of your lines. If you plan to color with markers right on your final drawing, be sure whatever pens you use are waterproof.

• **PEN TABLET (OPTIONAL):**
If you prefer to draw digitally, I highly recommend using a Wacom pen tablet.

1 PLANNING YOUR CHARACTER

Let's get started! In order to successfully create an original character, you need a plan before you begin your drawing. Here are some suggestions to get you thinking.

- **Name your character:**
Who is this character?

- **Make a word list:**
Pick a few words that describe your character. Think about both their physical appearance and personality.

- **Visualize your character:**
What does your character look like? Make a few quick sketches of ideas you have and write down some of your character's defining physical characteristics.

- **Clothing/accessories:**
If your character wears clothing, what does it look like? Does your character have different clothing for different activities?

- **Equipment:**
Does your character use any defining objects? Draw a few sketches of any equipment your character uses.

- **Build a world:**
Imagine the world your character will live in; jot down some ideas about where your character lives, locations your character might visit, and story ideas.

- **Get inspired:**
Look at great artwork you admire—but be sure you develop your own unique style!

My planning notes.

MY PLAN

I've decided to create a warrior character called a **Kagonin Knight**. He wears a powerful mega armor suit that gives him the strength to carry a large Siege Blade.

WORLD BUILDING

For me, as an artist and storyteller, a big part of my character design and development process is **world building**. Characters don't exist in a vacuum; for a character to live and breathe, it needs to be part of a world. I spend a great deal of time imagining the worlds my characters inhabit. On the back of each coloring page in this book, you'll see the profile I developed for each character. I could certainly draw characters without all this information, but thinking it through helps me create characters that are more than just drawings on a page—they are each part of a bigger story.

2 BUILDING THE FRAMEWORK

Before you start drawing your character, it's important to establish what's inside of it. Imagine there are wires inside your character, and draw its **internal framework**. In your sketches, identify all the most important parts of your character, such as key joints, head position, hips, arms, and legs, with simple shapes. These framework drawings are also called **armatures** or **gesture drawings**. Create several of these loose sketches of your character in different poses so you can understand your character's internal structure and how that affects how your character moves through space. The key at this stage is to work fast and draw lots of sketches; don't get too hung up on how well drawn they look. Once you have a favorite pose, use that sketch as a blueprint to follow as you construct your character in the next steps.

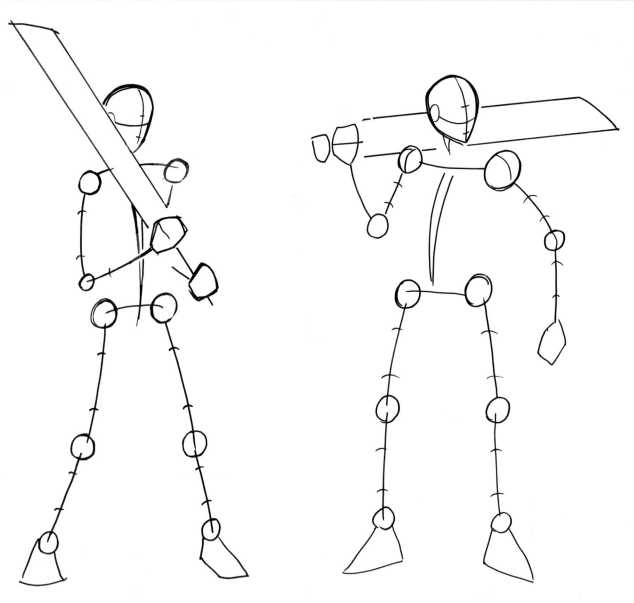

Quick framework sketches of different poses of the Kagonin Knight.

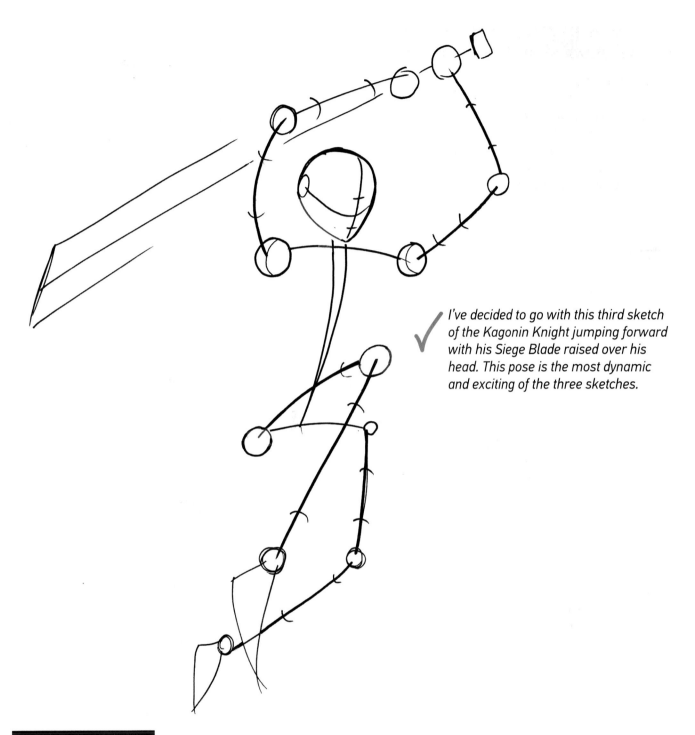

I've decided to go with this third sketch of the Kagonin Knight jumping forward with his Siege Blade raised over his head. This pose is the most dynamic and exciting of the three sketches.

KEEP IN MIND

Think of a drawing as something you craft. In order for it to be believable and well constructed, you will need to start by creating a strong internal structure. This is the most important part of your drawing. If your structure is weak, your character will be weak. If your structure is strong, it will easily be able to support the shapes and forms you will add to it in the next steps.

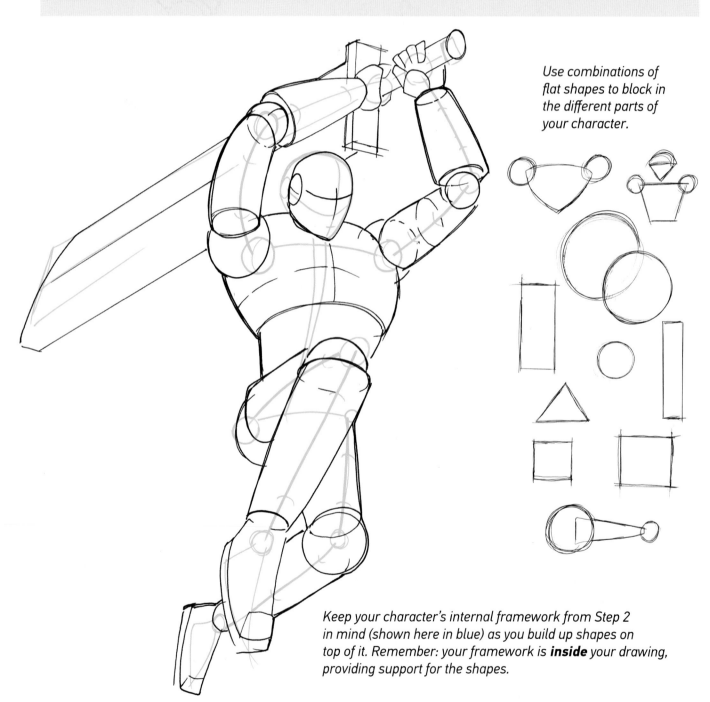

3 BLOCKING IN THE SHAPES

Now that you understand your character's pose, start blocking in large, flat shapes to indicate the head, body, arms, and legs. Remember, you're building all of this right onto the framework you established in Step 2. You can draw right on your framework drawing, or, if you have one, you can use a light table to draw on a new piece of paper with the framework drawing underneath. Remember that you're only using flat shapes in this step. They can have a hint of three-dimensional form, but it is most important at this stage to focus on blocking in the basic shapes.

Use combinations of flat shapes to block in the different parts of your character.

*Keep your character's internal framework from Step 2 in mind (shown here in blue) as you build up shapes on top of it. Remember: your framework is **inside** your drawing, providing support for the shapes.*

KEEP IN MIND

Make sure that when you are drawing your shapes you do not lose the essence of the framework. It's important at this step to also establish proper proportions in your character. Take your time to make sure that both arms and both legs are equal lengths and all the limbs connect to the framework properly.

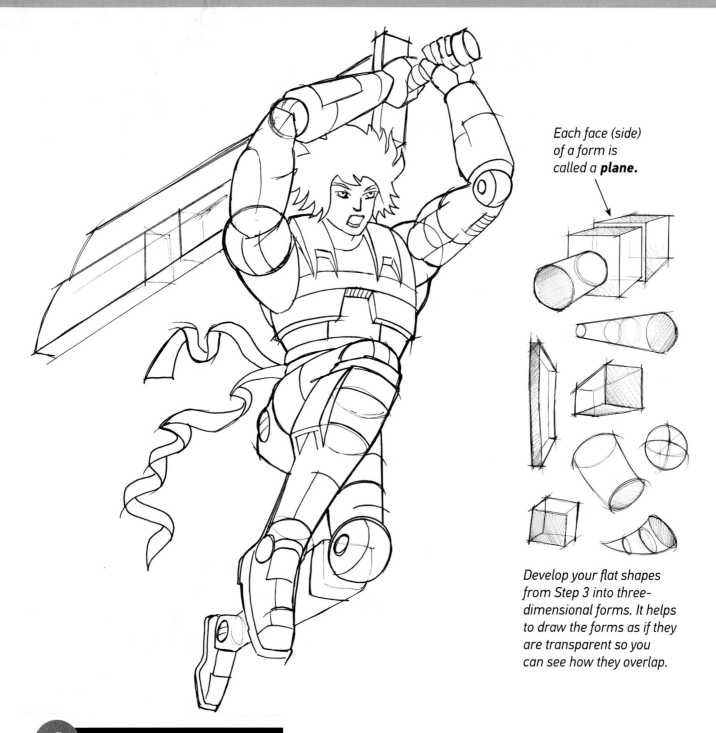

*Each face (side) of a form is called a **plane.***

Develop your flat shapes from Step 3 into three-dimensional forms. It helps to draw the forms as if they are transparent so you can see how they overlap.

4 DEFINING THE FORMS

Next, develop the flat shapes from Step 3 into three-dimensional shapes called **forms**. These forms are the building blocks of your character; they give your character volume and make it feel real. Think about how each form interlocks, overlaps, and intersects each surrounding form. In this step, draw all the forms of your character as if they are transparent so you can see through them to make sure each part fits together in a way that makes sense.

5 REFINING THE FORMS

Once you are happy with all the forms you built up in Step 4, you can continue to refine your drawing. Erase the lines that made your character's forms look transparent. Continue to build up details with smaller forms that pop off your character's surface. You'll know you're ready to move to Step 6 when your character feels very solid and looks complete to you.

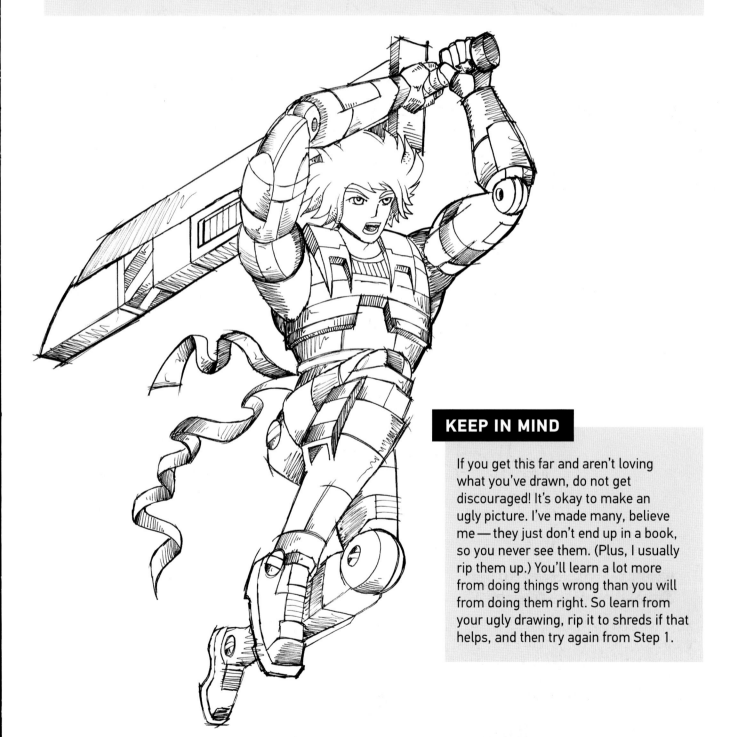

KEEP IN MIND

If you get this far and aren't loving what you've drawn, do not get discouraged! It's okay to make an ugly picture. I've made many, believe me — they just don't end up in a book, so you never see them. (Plus, I usually rip them up.) You'll learn a lot more from doing things wrong than you will from doing them right. So learn from your ugly drawing, rip it to shreds if that helps, and then try again from Step 1.

6 INKING

Once you are happy with your finished drawing from Step 5, you can create the final inked line drawing, either with black pens or digitally. Keep the original underlying forms in mind when you're inking these final lines. This is the stage to add any additional surface details as well. You can redraw your Step 5 drawing on a new sheet of paper if you want to save the drawing, but I usually ink right onto the final drawing and erase the pencil lines afterward.

7 ADDING COLOR: LIGHT SOURCE AND SHADING

Before getting started with color, it's important to identify your light source and understand how light falls on the forms of your character. A light source can be natural light from the sun or artificial light from a lamp. The key is to make sure all the forms are illuminated from a consistently positioned light source so all light that falls on your character is coming from the same direction. This will make your character feel solid and look believable.

Make a few copies of your inked drawing (or scan it so you can work digitally) and practice understanding light sources by shading your drawing with just gray tones. This is called a **tonal study**. Forget about color for a moment—instead, imagine your character as a three-dimensional model made out of white clay. How would the light fall on each form? Lighting from above makes a character look very different than lighting from below or from the side. Once you have a tonal study you like, you can use it as a guide for adding color to your inked drawing in the next few steps.

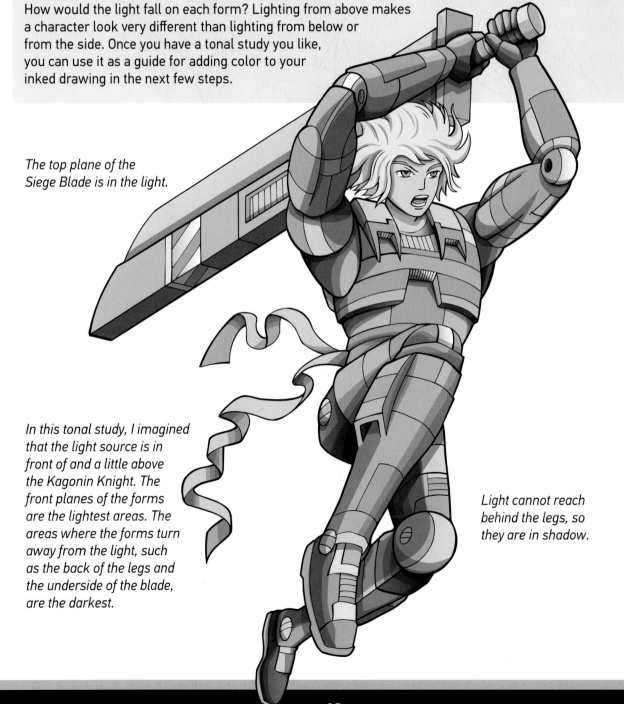

The top plane of the Siege Blade is in the light.

In this tonal study, I imagined that the light source is in front of and a little above the Kagonin Knight. The front planes of the forms are the lightest areas. The areas where the forms turn away from the light, such as the back of the legs and the underside of the blade, are the darkest.

Light cannot reach behind the legs, so they are in shadow.

8 ADDING COLOR: BLOCKING IN COLOR

The first step to coloring your character is deciding what colors you will use. Then, fill in each area with a few medium to light tones of your colors. For now, keep these base colors very simple, flat, and not too dark— you're not thinking about shadows or highlights yet, only blocking in what colors go in each area.

Use a few medium to light tones of your base colors.

KEEP IN MIND

Coloring is a very personal process; every artist has a favorite way to color. I love to work digitally, so I bring my final inked drawing from Step 6 into my computer and color it using a Wacom pen tablet in Adobe Illustrator and/or Photoshop. If you prefer to work with markers, paint, or other non-digital media, be sure to ink Step 6 on the kind of paper you like to color on; and, if you plan to use a wet medium like markers, be sure your black lines are drawn with a waterproof pen so they don't bleed. Even though I am using a digitally colored example here, the ideas of the lesson apply to any media you might work in. I spent many years working with markers, colored pencils, and oil paint using almost the exact same process of coloring that I now do digitally.

9 ADDING COLOR: GRADIENTS

Now that you have your color blocked in, it's time to begin giving your forms more dimension by adding **gradients**. Gradients are areas that blend softly across a color from light to dark to create a smooth color transition, and they should follow your character's forms. Refer back to your shaded drawing in Step 7 and use that as a guide for where your lights and darks should be. Darken areas in shadow with gradients that progress smoothly across each form, blending with the underlying base tones of color. You spent a lot of energy crafting your character out of three-dimensional forms.
Now it's time to use color, light, and shadow to enhance and accentuate those forms.

10 ADDING COLOR: SHADOWS ▼

Now it's time to deepen your shadows. Keep referring back to your tonal study from Step 7, and darken the areas where the light from your light source does not hit with deeper, darker shadows. Your character should look almost done and feel very solid now.

11 ADDING COLOR: HIGHLIGHTS ▶

All that's left to do is add highlights. These are subtle areas of a very light tone added to places where the light hits your character most directly. You can see how adding highlights in this step helps define the edges between forms, makes lighter areas pop, and adds a glossiness to the armor's surface. The Kagonin Knight is now complete!

KAGONIN KNIGHT

© Erik DePrince • www.mangatothemax.com

KIYA

UEE TROOPER

CLAUDE

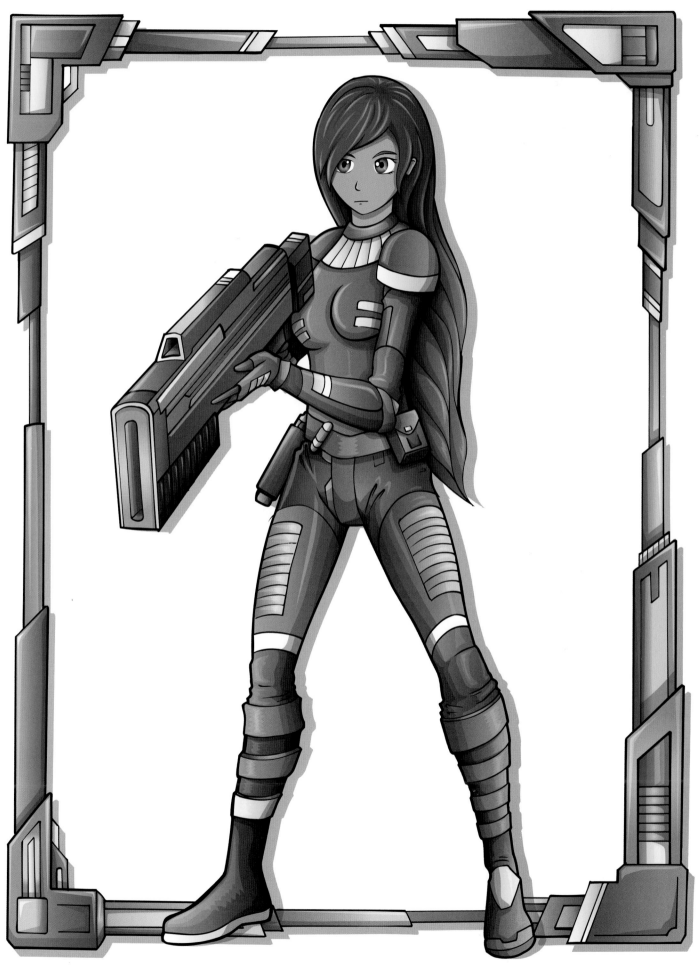

UEE General Patrol Reservist

COVERT WARRIOR

Kathryn

STATS

- Warrior Class: Psychic Dragon
- Physiology: Human-born Dragon Walker

SIZE:
- Human form: 5 ft. 3 in. (1.6 m) tall
- Dragon form: Small dragon, 15 ft. (4.57 m) long

OFFENSIVE CAPABILITIES:
- Human form: Hand-to-hand combat
- Dragon form: Strength

DEFENSIVE CAPABILITIES:
- Human form: Moderate armor
- Dragon form: Ability to create wormholes

PROFILE

One of the youngest Dragon Walkers, Si was the wife of a Japanese gangster in the 1960s. She and her husband were in New York City at a meeting with members of the Mafia when she died in a police raid. Three days later she awoke in the morgue, disoriented and confused. The morgue attendants watched, bewildered, as her broken body healed itself before their eyes. They called the police, and then it was only a matter of time before government agents arrived, kidnapping Si and transporting her to Area 51. There, scientists inflicted many painful injuries on Si to study her healing process. After years of this top-secret torture, she escaped in 1975.

Finally free, Si worked in the shadows as part of criminal groups, training in hand-to-hand combat and stealth fighting, determined never to be in a position of weakness or to be captured again. Many years later, the United Earth Enforcement (UEE) approached her. They told her they knew what she really was and wanted to work with her. She still had deep resentment toward government entities, but she listened, curious to learn more about herself. The UEE explained that she was a Dragon Walker and that they could teach her to shift into dragon form. They wanted her for a special ops group whose mission was to find and rescue covert operatives who had been left behind on other planets. As someone who had once been a lost secret herself, the mission was appealing, as was the training the UEE promised. Si agreed to join and became the first Dragon Walker to work directly with the UEE.

REGENERATING
SCALES

▲ **SI'S DRAGON FORM** (above)

Si can shift into dragon form and create wormholes in space, allowing her to travel great distances in secret while searching for covert operatives in distress.

STATS

- Warrior Class: UEE Special Ops
- Physiology: Earth-born human with extended lifespan
- Size: 6 ft. 2 in. (1.88 m)
- Offensive Capabilities: Hand-to-hand combat, Holographic Pulse Pistol
- Defensive Capabilities: Light armor, natural toughness

PROFILE

A famous war hero, Bulldog Carter has been an active soldier for more than 50 years thanks to anti-aging treatment from the UEE. The treatment includes a rare, difficult-to-produce serum, which the UEE is all too happy to provide in order to ensure Carter remains the public's popular hero. Carter runs a special ops unit called the Bulldogs who go undercover to stop criminal organizations from smuggling dangerous items onto Earth. When they occasionally seize new technology, they hand it over to the Guardian Captains. The Bulldogs' experience also makes them the unit to turn to when help is needed to locate kidnapped officials.

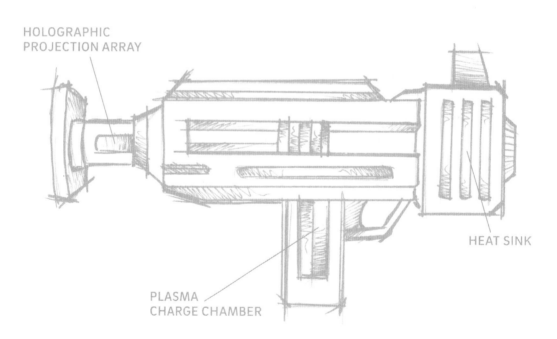

HOLOGRAPHIC
PROJECTION ARRAY

HEAT SINK

PLASMA
CHARGE CHAMBER

▲ HOLOGRAPHIC PULSE PISTOL *(above)*

Though Carter's fame has been quite an asset for the UEE's public relations, they understand that having such a widely recognizable face is not always helpful when conducting covert missions. So the UEE created a special extra-large high-velocity pulse pistol that has a customizable holographic projector embedded inside it. This invention allows Captain Carter to change his face at will when he has contact with it. The pistol is DNA responsive, so only he can use it.

STATS

- Warrior Class: UEE Covert Ops
- Physiology: Earth-born human
- Size: 5 ft. 1 in. (1.55 m)
- Offensive Capabilities: Agility, dexterity, hand-to-hand combat
- Defensive Capabilities: Agility, Alien Arachnid Silk Boots

PROFILE

Kiya came from a well-known family of gymnasts, though she never had a chance to follow in her parents' footsteps. When she was a young child, right after the United Empires (UE) visited and departed Earth, her family left Earth on a ship that was part of a diplomatic envoy sent after the UE's ships. Along with many others, Kiya's family felt strongly that Earth's survival depended on being part of the UE. But it was a poorly planned endeavor that took a tragic turn when the envoy was attacked by what salvagers later determined was a dragon. Kiya's family's ship crashed on an asteroid, where they encountered dozens of dangerous alien ghost spiders. They fought and killed many, but in the end, only Kiya survived by hiding in the wreckage until a rescue team arrived. As the sole survivor of her family, all the cargo and salvageable items on the ship, including the very valuable ghost spider carcasses, belonged to her.

Kiya now works for the UEE as a secret agent specializing in sabotage and theft. Super nimble and stealthy, her genetic disposition toward acrobatics makes her highly proficient in martial arts and sword fighting. Her work with the UEE gives her a sense of purpose after the tragic loss of her family.

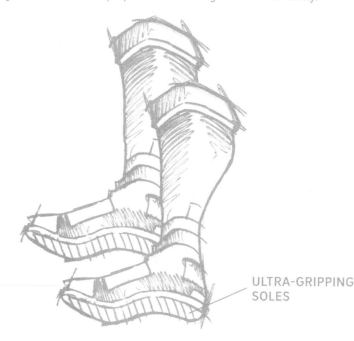

ULTRA-GRIPPING SOLES

▲ **ALIEN ARACHNID SILK BOOTS** *(above)*

Kiya had custom boots made from the dead ghost spiders' silk. The silk gives the boots anti-gravity properties that allow Kiya to experience one quarter of any gravity wherever she goes, enabling her to jump very high and move very quickly.

STATS

- Warrior Class: Plasma Elemental Dragon
- Physiology: Human-born Dragon Walker

SIZE:
- Human form: 5 ft. 6 in. (1.68 m) tall
- Dragon form: Small dragon, 12 ft. (3.66 m) long

OFFENSIVE CAPABILITIES:
- Human form: Spectral Blaster
- Dragon form: Spectral Breath

DEFENSIVE CAPABILITIES:
- Human form: Healing Armor
- Dragon form: Regenerating Scales

PROFILE

A Viking from the year 700, Reya is the oldest Dragon Walker on Earth. She was a shield maiden who died while invading a village in what would later become Russia. During the invasion, everyone had died on both sides, leaving no survivors. Reya awoke to witness her injuries quickly healing, but she clearly remembered dying. Right as the final wound closed, she burst into dragon form. She believed she had taken the form of Eir, the Norse goddess of healing. She spent the next several years living in dragon form in the mountains. Unlike many Dragon Walkers that came later, Reya remembered everything about her life prior to dying. One day, when she was near her old village, she abruptly changed back into human form, as she didn't yet understand how to control the transformation. She told her tale to her village, but no one believed her; they blamed her for the deaths of her warrior group and cast her out of the village.

Like all Dragon Walkers, Reya doesn't age, so she had to move and change her identity every ten or fifteen years. For a while she worked as an antiques dealer, then as an author of Viking fairytales and stories about dragons. She eventually heard of Claude's League of Dragon Walkers, but after so long alone, she saw little need to join a group. However, that changed after the mass arrival of other dragons on Earth; suddenly, being alone felt dangerous. She reluctantly decided to join the League.

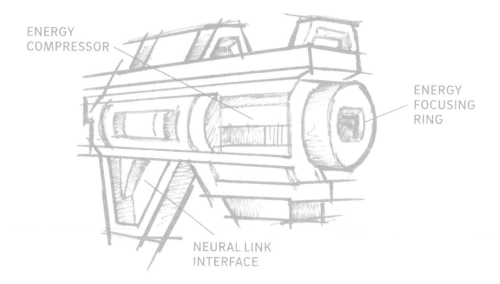

ENERGY COMPRESSOR

ENERGY FOCUSING RING

NEURAL LINK INTERFACE

▲ SPECTRAL BLASTER *(above)*

One main reason Reya decided to join the League was to benefit from the cybernetic technology they had developed. While in dragon form—but not while in human form—she can shoot a beam of light energy from her mouth. The League developed a neurally linked blaster to allow her to use her dragon energy beam while in human form.

STATS

- Warrior Class: UEE Sword Master
- Physiology: Earth-born human with cybernetic implants
- Size: 6 ft. 4 in. (1.93 m)
- Offensive Capabilities: Sword fighting
- Defensive Capabilities: Sword fighting, Alien Arachnid Silk Cape

PROFILE

Captain Clark lost his arms in the same battle that injured Kente, the UEE Strategic Commander and foremost professor of hand-to-hand combat at the UEE Academy. Before the injury, Captain Clark was one of Kente's best students and the only warrior to have ever earned the title of UEE Sword Grand Master. After his injury, the UEE provided Captain Clark with their most advanced bionic arms, which he quickly mastered. The arms are a huge attribute for a sword master; thanks to their incredible strength, Captain Clark can now deftly wield a Siege Blade, a weapon most warriors cannot even lift. For defensive protection, he wears a cape made of alien arachnid silk which is like a fabric shield; when pulled across his body, it protects him like a sheet of armor.

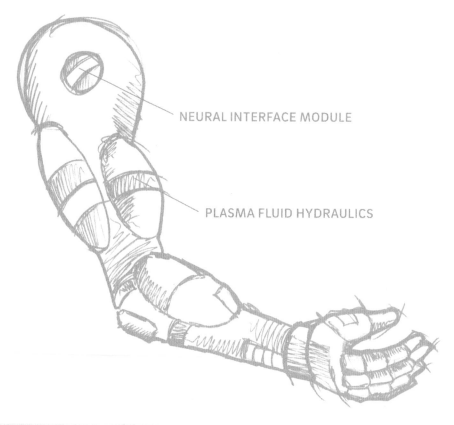

NEURAL INTERFACE MODULE

PLASMA FLUID HYDRAULICS

▲ **BIONIC ARMS** *(above)*

Captain Clark's Bionic Arms allow him to lift incredibly heavy objects and wield the largest Siege Blades, making him the ideal warrior to work with the largest UEE robots.

STATS

- Warrior Class: UEE Guardian
- Physiology: Earth-born human
- Size: 6 ft. (1.83 m) or taller
- Offensive Capabilities: Siege Blade, strength
- Defensive Capabilities: Mega Armor Suit, nanobot healing technology

PROFILE

The most elite humans in the UEE, Kagonin Knights face rigorous mental and physical training to perfect their abilities. Their entire being is dedicated to protecting Earth's newly developed technologies. Knights are volunteers who are not allowed to have any attachments to family; they must be alone in the world. Equipped with a mechanized Mega Armor Suit controlled by a neural interface, the Kagonin Knights are known as a very tough, battle-hardened group, unwaveringly loyal to the UEE. As the protectors of Earth's technology, Kagonin Knights do not interact with it or know much about it; they simply guard it with their lives.

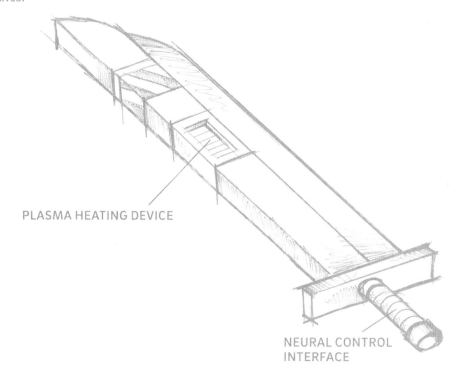

PLASMA HEATING DEVICE

NEURAL CONTROL INTERFACE

▲ MEGA ARMOR SUIT AND SIEGE BLADE *(above)*

The Mega Armor Suit is worn over the body like an exoskeleton and doubles the wearer's stamina while also increasing their strength by tenfold. The suit allows Kagonin Knights to wield the feared Siege Blade, which, because of its size and weight, normally only large robots like Urban Ground Defenders (UGDs) can control. Inside the suit are many systems, including medical nanobots specifically designed to continuously repair the wearer's body. Thanks to these nanobots, Knights do not age while wearing the suit. Each Knight must spend months of mental training to hone their ability to connect with the suit's neural interface. Continuing to perfect this connection is an ongoing pursuit for Knights; the better Knights are at controlling the connection, the better they are at using the suit as a powerful extension of their bodies.

STATS

SATEENA
- Warrior Class: UEE Special Ops
- Physiology: Genetically modified synthetic human
- Size: 5 ft. 7 in. (1.7 m)
- Offensive Capabilities: Crossbow, sword fighting
- Defensive Capabilities: Moderate Regenerating Armor

ZAYLORE
- Warrior Class: UEE Special Ops
- Physiology: Genetically modified synthetic dragon
- Size: Small dragon, 12 ft. (3.66 m) long
- Offensive Capabilities: Claws, powerful jaws
- Defensive Capabilities: Heavy Regenerating Armor and Regenerating Scales

PROFILE

Sateena is the result of recent UEE genetic engineering experiments that spliced human and dragon DNA into a synthetically created human body. Because her growth was accelerated to the age of 20 in a very short period of time, Sateena has few real memories or experiences, so she was given genetic memories of combat training, accelerated learning abilities, and an elongated lifespan. Despite her powerful combat potential, she is still very young and inexperienced, eager to learn about her abilities and make sense of her uniqueness.

The UEE also created a "brother" for Sateena. She was raised alongside a genetically engineered dragon named Zaylore who was created using some of her human DNA. His body is composed of an experimental organic-based metal material, allowing his cybernetic implants to grow as he grows. He has the potential to grow to more than 120 ft. (36.6 m) long.

Sateena and Zaylore share a powerful psychic link with one another, allowing them to communicate over vast distances. In fact, scientists believe there is no physical limit to their communication range. This bond is being called a Transdimensional Psychic Connection, something no one has ever seen before. In addition to their psychic link, the pair can also physically switch bodies, something they have not told anyone about. Though they both officially pledge their allegiance to the UEE, their only true loyalties are to each other.

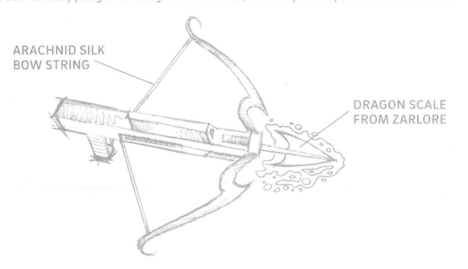

ARACHNID SILK BOW STRING

DRAGON SCALE FROM ZARLORE

▲ **SATEENA'S CROSSBOW** *(above)*

Sateena uses a life-draining bow designed by the UEE to battle large organic creatures, aliens, and even dragons. The bow's rare arrows are made of scales taken from the fire elemental dragon Zarlore. Very few of these arrows exist, so they must be recovered when used.

STATS

- Warrior Class: UEE Assault Trooper
- Physiology: Earth-born human
- Size: 5 ft. 6 in. to 6 ft. (1.68 to 1.83 m) or taller
- Offensive Capabilities: Hand-to-hand combat
- Defensive Capabilities: Agility, Alien Arachnid Silk Armor

PROFILE

The UEE has many Teleportation Combat Centers located around the globe that they use to teleport groups of soldiers to remote locations both on and off Earth. Typically when someone teleports, they experience five to ten seconds of extreme disorientation upon arriving at the destination, which leaves them vulnerable to enemy attack. UEE Ship Raiders train extensively to overcome this disorientation so they can immediately engage in combat after transport. Teleportation is frequently used to get troops onto enemy ships, so Ship Raiders are also trained to fight in tight places. The Acrobatic Evasion Training Program teaches Raiders how to scale a ship's walls and use a ship's confined environment to evade the enemy. Each Raider wears a custom-made, lightly armored Alien Arachnid Silk suit. These suits are extremely lightweight yet provide excellent protection from small arms fire, allowing the Raiders to be very agile and quick.

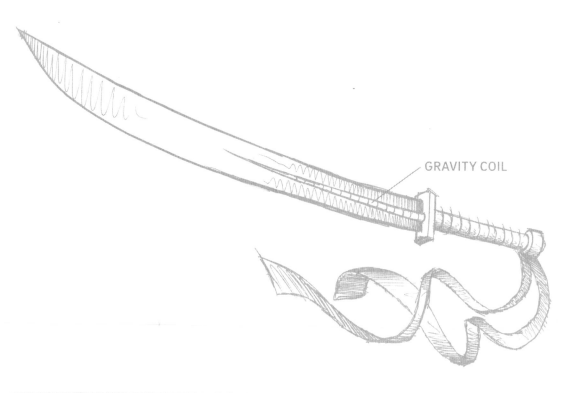

GRAVITY COIL

▲ SWIFT SWORD *(above)*

A Ship Raider's Swift Sword has a gravity coil that runs up the middle of it. This coil make the sword feel lighter than it is for increased agility in different gravity conditions. It also auto-adjusts the sword's weight and center of gravity for optimal handling during unusual evasive movements, such as fighting while upside down.

STATS

- Warrior Class: UEE Covert Ops
- Physiology: Earth-born human
- Size: 6 ft. (1.83 m)
- Offensive Capabilities: Hand-to-hand combat
- Defensive Capabilities: Light armor, EMP Boots

PROFILE

Prince Steel is a descendent of Chinese royalty. During the early 2100s, his family built a steel empire, and though the monarchy has long been gone, he took on the name Prince Steel, which started as a childhood nickname.

The UEE purchased most of the large companies after the world's countries fused. When his father died, Prince Steel finally accepted the UEE's standing offer to buy out his family's company, an offer that his father had long declined. Having lived in a gilded world all his life, Prince Steel longed to get out in the universe and do something adventurous, so as part of the buyout, he negotiated a deal for an ambassadorial position for himself. He is now one of Earth's few Interplanetary Ambassadors. As part of the deal, he also managed to keep control of a small, covert scientific group to develop advanced armor technologies for the UEE. Officially, he travels to different worlds in the Empires to represent the UEE, while unofficially he is also operating as a spy, using his voyages to other worlds as opportunities to gather intelligence and acquire technology for his secret armor research.

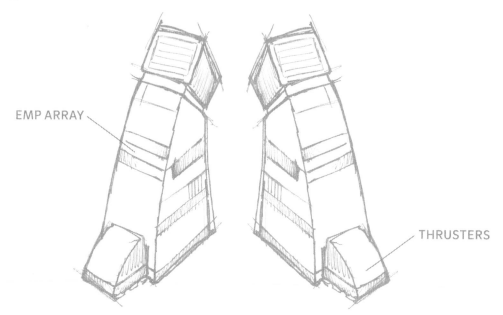

EMP ARRAY

THRUSTERS

▲ EMP BOOTS (above)

Prince Steel's boots are designed to emit high-intensity EMP bursts in a small area that can disrupt computer equipment and scramble communications. The burst is optimized to be most effective against small, close-range targets, so it does not work as well against large, heavily shielded robots. The boots are also armored and have small thrusters on the soles to allow limited flight over short distances and increased jumping abilities.

STATS

- Warrior Class: UEE Special Ops
- Physiology: Genetically engineered human
- Size: 6 ft. (1.83 m) or taller
- Offensive Capabilities: Dragon Claw Blades
- Defensive Capabilities: Cloaking Skin, Dragon Claw Blades

PROFILE

Blade Jumpers are a UEE special ops unit used during invasions for sabotage, abduction, and other stealthy missions. Jumpers are the only unit that is genetically engineered en masse. They are similar to clones, but not always genetically identical to one another. Blade Jumpers are created by splicing together human and dragon DNA. One of the benefits of this combination is their scaled Cloaking Skin. Though it looks like normal human skin, their skin is actually covered in miniscule, translucent scales too small to see with the eye. These scales allow Jumpers to cloak themselves to become nearly invisible at will and make their skin far more durable than human skin. The Blade Jumper unit is controlled and trained by the cyborg Kentar, whose unique fighting style is built around the Dragon Claw Blades that Jumpers wear on their arms.

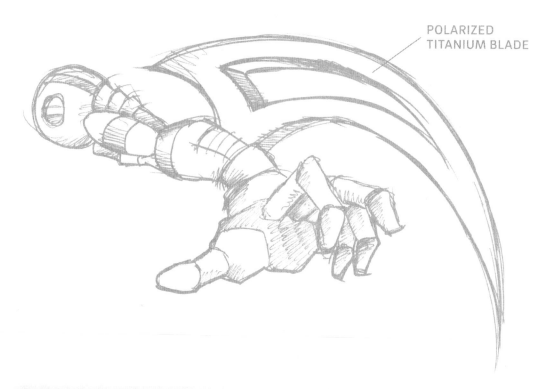

POLARIZED
TITANIUM BLADE

▲ DRAGON CLAW BLADES *(above)*

Jumpers do not use blasters; instead they prefer stealthy weapons like Dragon Claw Blades, which are reinforced, polarized titanium blades that can slice through almost any material. Designed to rip through any kind of door, the claws are very lightweight for their size and strength, allowing for close combat melee and speed. Because of their size, they can also function defensively as shields against small arms fire.

STATS

- Warrior Class: UEE Trooper
- Physiology: Earth-born human
- Size: 5 ft. to 6 ft. (1.52 to 1.83 m)
- Offensive Capabilities: Thunder Sword
- Defensive Capabilities: Heavy armor

PROFILE

Thunder Sword Warriors are a common trooper unit of the UEE. They are excellent for close-range fighting and can be placed with almost any other troop, making them extremely versatile warriors. Completely un-augmented, they wear heavy armor and rely entirely on their skills with the Thunder Sword.

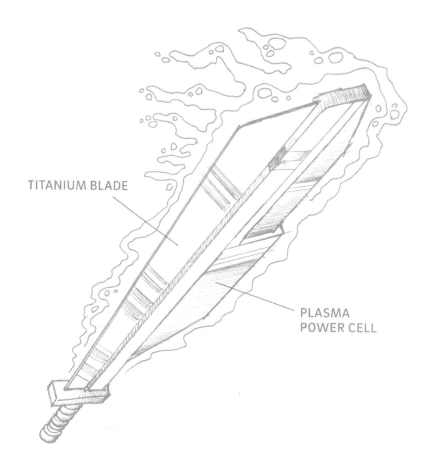

TITANIUM BLADE

PLASMA
POWER CELL

▲ **THUNDER SWORD** *(above)*

The Thunder Sword is a smaller, lighter version of the Siege Blade. Like the Siege Blade, it can heat up and melt metal, but it is not as heavy or powerful as what the Kagonin Knights and Urban Ground Defender (UGD) robots carry. The sword earns its name from the sounds it makes when it hits an object. Since the Thunder Sword has less insulation and armor than the Siege Blade, the plasma is more exposed inside the blade, and it makes a thunderous sound when it strikes something.

STATS

- Warrior Class: Psychic Dragon
- Physiology: Human-born Dragon Walker

SIZE:
- Human form: 6 ft. 2 in. (1.88 m) tall
- Dragon form: Small dragon, 14 ft. (4.27 m) long

OFFENSIVE CAPABILITIES:
- Human form: Regulator Sword
- Dragon form: Psychic abilities, claws

DEFENSIVE CAPABILITIES:
- Human form: Heavy armor
- Dragon form: Regenerating Scales

PROFILE

Originally from Australia, Theo died fighting in Belgium during World War I. He was reborn just hours later in the middle of the battlefield, with absolutely no memory of who he was or what had happened. Disoriented and frantic, he was quickly taken prisoner by the Germans. It was only through his interrogations over the ensuing two years that he learned his name and identity. Theo stayed amazingly healthy while imprisoned, surviving easily on hardly any food, which baffled his captors.

After the war ended, Theo went back to the life that he had lived before the war, but as his memories never returned, he felt like an imposter in someone else's life. He soon began having vivid, terrifying dreams about dragons. He dreamed he could move things with his mind, and then discovered he could actually do so while awake. Seeing no point in continuing to live what felt like a false life, Theo decided to embrace his new identity. He took a new name, Ronin, and set out in search of answers, traveling the world looking for others like him, or at least some peace. Eventually his travels brought him to Tibet, where he lived a quiet, meditative life, revered as a mystical figure, for hundreds of years. But all that changed the day Claude arrived at Ronin's temple. Ronin had seen Claude coming to him in a dream and knew he, too, was different. Claude asked Ronin to join the League of Dragon Walkers, an offer Ronin gladly accepted. Ronin's patience had paid off: the answers he had sought for so long had finally found him.

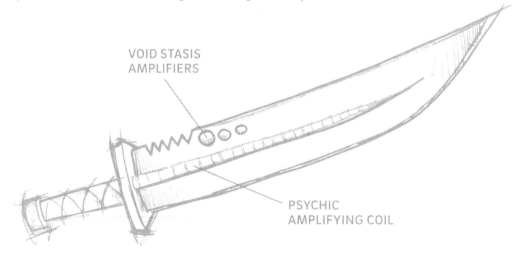

VOID STASIS
AMPLIFIERS

PSYCHIC
AMPLIFYING COIL

▲ **THE REGULATOR** *(above)*

Ronin uses his sword, the Regulator, a gift from Claude, to amplify his psychic and telekinetic abilities while in human form. It helps him move large objects with his mind and create void bubbles, which he can usually only make while in his dragon form.

STATS

- Warrior Class: UEE Guardian
- Physiology: Earth-born human with extended lifespan
- Size: 6 ft. (1.83 m) or taller
- Offensive Capabilities: Hand-to-hand combat, sword fighting, nonlethal Pulse Stunner
- Defensive Capabilities: Alien Arachnid Silk Armor

PROFILE

Guardian Captains are known as the curators of Earth's technology. Because of the great importance of this task, the UEE is careful to select recruits that they feel will be loyal to Earth above all else. Unlike the Kagonin Knights, whose sole purpose is to protect technology without interacting with it, Guardian Captains must know everything there is to know about the technology, including how it works and the locations of every special piece of technology on the planet. It is their job to organize, curate, and safeguard this vital information. Guardian Captains also go on missions to retrieve stolen items, protect Earth against malicious technology that might be smuggled in, and work to acquire new technology from off-world.

Though naturally born humans, all Guardian Captains undergo a genetic therapy after they are born to give them longer life. Each has the exact same rank of captain. The UEE made them officers so that at any time, if a situation arises, they can lead a platoon or battalion of any other UEE soldiers.

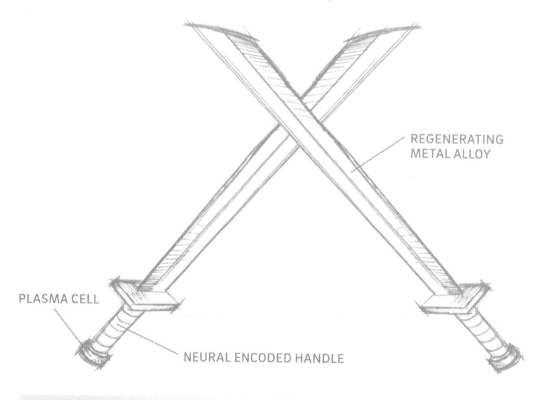

REGENERATING METAL ALLOY

PLASMA CELL

NEURAL ENCODED HANDLE

▲ BLAZE SWORDS *(above)*

The Guardian Captain's Blaze Swords have a plasma fuel cell inside the handle, which heats up and electrifies the sword.

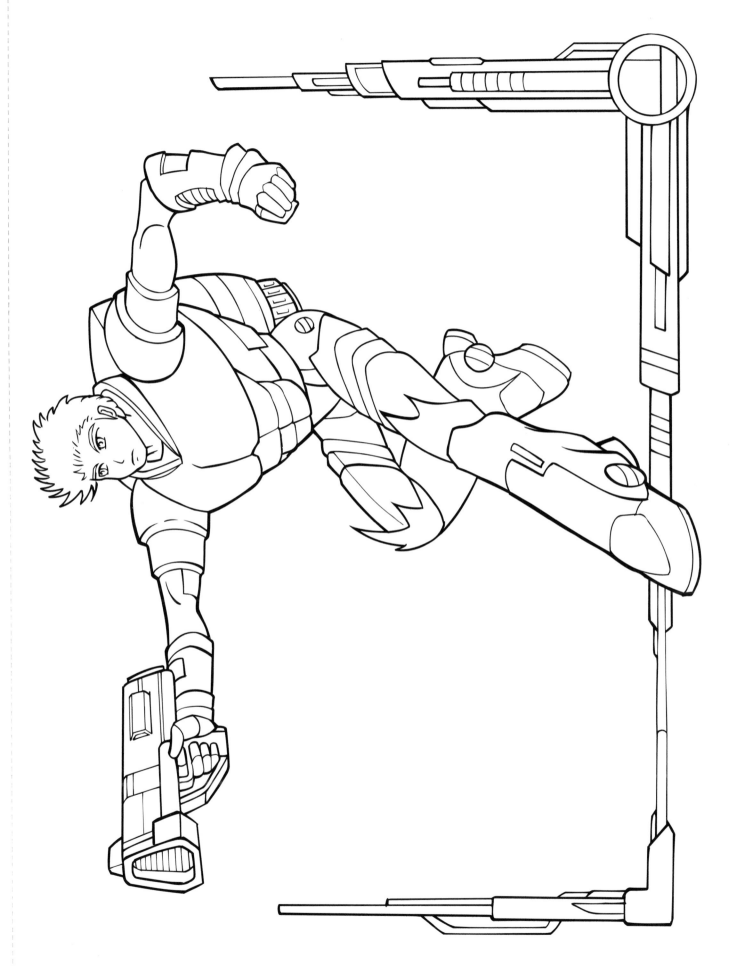

STATS

- Warrior Class: UEE Trooper
- Physiology: Earth-born human
- Size: 5 ft. to 6 ft. (1.52 to 1.83 m)
- Offensive Capabilities: Plasma Pistol Cutter
- Defensive Capabilities: Heavy armor

PROFILE

With the threat of other Empires now real, there is no need for a draft on Earth. Everyone wants to serve, so there is no lack of volunteers; with so many applicants, many citizens actually get turned away. Airborne Sergeants are one of the most basic, standardized units requiring no special skills or genetic engineering, making them one of the most applied-for positions. Specifically trained for physical infiltration of ships, these warriors secure a safe entry point for other troops to pass through.

Airborne Sergeants use zero gravity space suits. Their head is covered by a small force field when jumping out of drop ships, enabling them to perform high-altitude, high-velocity jumps. They also specialize in ship-to-ship raids in space, able to jump from a drop ship into or onto other ships.

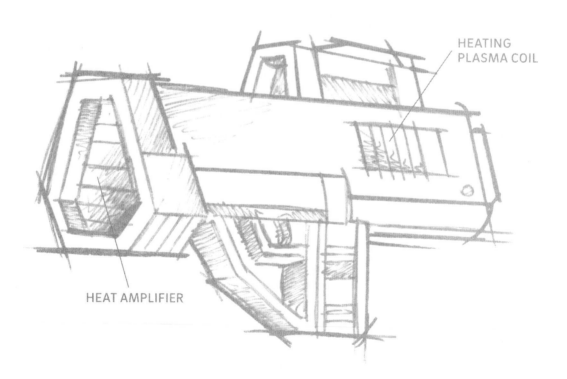

HEATING
PLASMA COIL

HEAT AMPLIFIER

▲ PLASMA PISTOL CUTTER *(above)*

All Airborne Sergeants are issued a specially designed multifunction plasma blaster that can be used as a ranged field weapon. It also serves as a metal cutting tool and welder, designed to breach spaceship hulls by cutting through almost any type of metal and also seal the hole up again.

STATS

- Warrior Class: Warrior/Psychic Dragon
- Physiology: Human-born Dragon Walker

SIZE:
- Human form: 5 ft. 3 in. (1.6 m) tall
- Dragon form: Medium dragon, 25 ft. (7.62 m) long

OFFENSIVE CAPABILITIES:
- Human form: Magma Charge Pistol
- Dragon form: Massive Claws

DEFENSIVE CAPABILITIES:
- Human form: Manipulation, moderate armor
- Dragon form: Regenerating Scales

PROFILE

Jane was the resourceful daughter of a settler family who died at the hands of bandits in the 1840s while traveling across the United States. Jane awoke shortly after she died; without being able to explain it, she knew she had died. She remembered her family and the bandits, but not much else. Jane had always been a very persuasive young woman, but after she died, this skill was incredibly enhanced. At the first town she came to after her rebirth, she found she could influence people's memories and shape their perspective about events. She put this powerful psychic ability to work by manipulating people to give her exactly what she needed, and then she made them forget all about her.

Jane had always been a pretty good shot, so she decided to become a gunslinger. This way, she figured, she could protect herself, make some money, and maybe even find the bandits who had killed her family. Over time, as the United States became more modern, so too did Wild Jane. Eventually she settled down and became a historian, writer, and antiques dealer of old western-style pistols. When dragons arrived on Earth, Jane decided she was done with hiding and came out to the UEE and the public about her identity and story. She now works with the UEE training soldiers in marksmanship. She is considered by many to be the best quick-draw gunslinger on Earth, and her persuasion skills have become so powerful that she can even influence other Dragon Walkers, who are typically immune to psychic abilities.

LASER SIGHT

MAGMA CHARGES

▲ MAGMA CHARGE PISTOL (above)

The Magma Charge Pistol is Jane's own invention. Inside the weapon's frame is a Western-style revolver. The lead charges are superheated by a plasma pulse as they are fired, which is why she gave the gun its name—it literally shoots red-hot lead.

STATS

- Warrior Class: UEE Trooper
- Physiology: Earth-born human
- Size: 5 ft. to 6 ft. (1.52 to 1.83 m)
- Offensive Capabilities: Patrol Plasma Rifle
- Defensive Capabilities: Light armor

PROFILE

The UEE General Patrol Reservists are a common, versatile unit. They undergo general combat training and are lightly armored. Typically they rotate into domestic positions on Earth such as general guard duty, crowd control, and large event security, where they work alongside UEE Security Force Guard Unit robots. Made up entirely of part-time soldiers, the Patrol Reservists are the perfect unit for people who have dedicated themselves to other careers but still want to do their part to serve Earth.

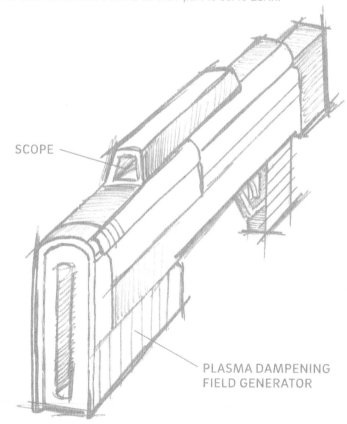

SCOPE

PLASMA DAMPENING
FIELD GENERATOR

▲ **PATROL PLASMA RIFLE** *(above)*

The Patrol Plasma Rifle is a basic weapon that can change from nonlethal to lethal with the flick of a switch. In nonlethal mode, it releases a shockwave burst that can stun organic beings, incapacitating them for about five minutes. In lethal mode, the rifle shoots plasma bursts that destroy both organic and mechanical targets.

STATS

- Warrior Class: Shape-shifting Dragon Warrior
- Physiology: Human-born Dragon Walker with cybernetic upgrades

SIZE:
- Human form: 5 ft. 10 in. (1.78 m) tall
- Dragon form: Small dragon, 12 ft. (3.66 m) long

OFFENSIVE CAPABILITIES:
- Human form: Hand-to-hand combat, archery
- Dragon form: Claws

DEFENSIVE CAPABILITIES:
- Human form: Light armor
- Dragon form: Regenerating Scales

PROFILE

Kathryn lived during the Victorian Age in Russia and died in the late 1800s when her family's village was destroyed by a fire. She awoke among the ashes, confused and terrified. Shortly after that, she began having vivid dreams of being a dragon. She tried to convince herself they were nightmares from surviving the fire, but she knew in her heart it was something more. Whenever she got very emotional or angry, she would feel a physical burning sensation that she always worked desperately to calm. But one day, tired of fighting herself, she let the burning continue until her whole body felt like it was on fire; then it *was* on fire, and she transformed into a dragon, just like in her dreams. It was the most powerful freedom she had ever experienced.

Kathryn spent many years traveling the world as smuggler, first of illegal weapons and later of technology. She had no fear of rival smugglers; after all, no one could hurt her. She had already died once, and she knew that at any point she could channel her anger into transformation. As the world advanced, so did she. She taught herself cybernetics and learned how to create her own implants to help enhance her abilities. When she met Claude and learned of the League of Dragon Walkers, he was very impressed with her skills, so he put her in charge of cybernetics within the League. Thanks to her skills, many Dragon Walkers now enjoy customized cybernetic upgrades without having to work with the UEE.

HYPER-INTELLIGENCE

▲ **KATHRYN'S DRAGON FORM** (above)

Though naturally very intelligent, in dragon form Kathryn becomes hyper-intelligent, able to solve problems and make cybernetic advancements with ease.

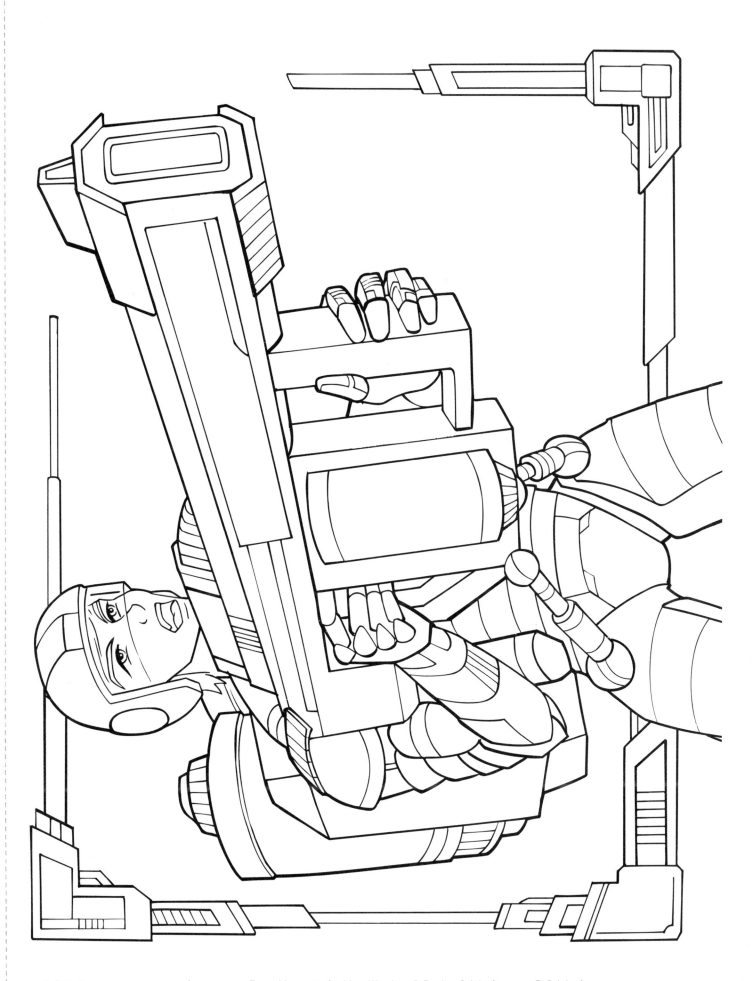

STATS

- Warrior Class: UEE Specialized Trooper
- Physiology: Earth-born human
- Size: 6 ft. (1.83 m) or taller
- Offensive Capabilities: Acid Launcher
- Defensive Capabilities: Moderate armor

PROFILE

A highly specialized troop class, Acid Throwers are each equipped with an Acid Launcher, a dangerous weapon that shoots an acid that dissolves most metals, making it incredibly effective against mechanized units such as robots and cyborgs. These destructive units are heavily armored because they tend to be singled out and targeted by opponents. In every platoon there is always at least one Acid Thrower soldier.

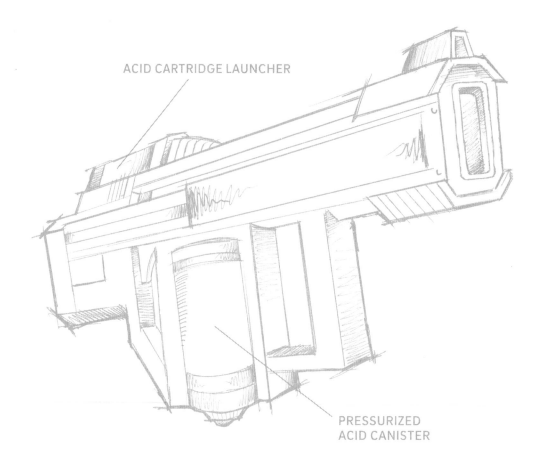

ACID CARTRIDGE LAUNCHER

PRESSURIZED
ACID CANISTER

▲ **ACID LAUNCHER** (above)

The Acid Launcher shoots acid bubble cartridges that burst when they hit their target, much like water balloons. The liquid inside is highly pressurized and each cartridge is very small, which allows each Launcher to have a capacity of one hundred compressed rounds.

STATS

- Warrior Class: UEE Hero
- Physiology: Earth-born human with genetic enhancements
- Size: 5 ft. 3 in. (1.6 m)
- Offensive Capabilities: Hand-to-hand combat, robot companions
- Defensive Capabilities: Moderate armor

PROFILE

Karlak Lordaz was originally an American solider from the mid-2100s who worked covertly for the CIA to eliminate secret targets. Because of his unique and valuable skills, he was given the opportunity to take anti-aging gene therapy as soon as it was available. By the UEE's estimates, he is now more than 150 years old, but no official files exist on him, and he has no known friends or family. The people who need him simply know him, and they also know he has a particular hatred for any creature not of Earth.

POLARIZED
TITANIUM ARMOR

BLAZE SWORD

▲ ROBOT 1 AND ROBOT 2 *(above)*

Karlak works with two outdated prototype robots that never went into mass production because of a software issue with their morality programming. Karlak rescued the robots from destruction and personally salvaged the program by rewriting it to serve his own needs. These two prototypes have been his companions ever since; like him, they do not age and, because he programmed them himself, he feels he can trust them unconditionally.

STATS

- Warrior Class: UEE Covert Ops
- Physiology: Earth-born human
- Size: 5 ft. to 6 ft. (1.52 to 1.83 m)
- Offensive Capabilities: Plasma Bow
- Defensive Capabilities: Light armor

PROFILE

Developed specifically as the only unit capable of using the powerful Plasma Bow, Covert Artillery unit volunteers undergo rigorous special training; only half of those who start will make it all the way through the program. Plasma Bows are very difficult for the average human to pull, and with exposed plasma running along the bow and arrows, they are also extremely hot and dangerous to handle, so all Covert Artillery soldiers have custom-made bionic arms installed. With an array of different arrows that range from Plasma Burn arrows to Acid arrows, the Plasma Bows are versatile and quiet, perfect for the small skirmishes the Covert Artillery often find themselves in.

HEAT SINK

POLARIZED
TITANIUM ARMOR

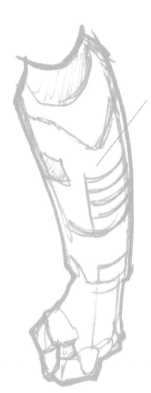

▲ **BIONIC INSULATED ARMS** *(above)*

Created by the UEE specifically to be used with the Plasma Bow, the Covert Artillery's Bionic Insulated Arms provide the extra strength needed to use the Plasma Bow with ease, while also protecting Artillery members from the energy released by the exposed plasma.

STATS

- Warrior Class: Warrior Dragon
- Physiology: Human-born Dragon Walker with cybernetic upgrades

SIZE:
- Human form: 6 ft. 6 in. (1.98 m) tall
- Dragon form: Small dragon, 16 ft. (4.88 m) long

OFFENSIVE CAPABILITIES:
- Human form: Hand-to-hand combat
- Dragon form: Claws

DEFENSIVE CAPABILITIES:
- Human form: Heavy armor
- Dragon form: Heavy Regenerating Armor, thick scales

PROFILE

Marcus was a well-known Wall Street prodigy in the 1980s. He ran his own financial firm and enjoyed a lavish lifestyle that included a private plane and many homes around the world. On a trip to one of his homes in Alaska in 1989, the plane he was piloting crashed into the mountains, killing him. Three weeks later, he was reborn, buried in the snow. Like Reya, the first Dragon Walker, he remembered everything about his previous life. Stunned, he headed on foot toward Anchorage. As cold as it was, he wasn't bothered by the temperature, and as the days passed, he ate nothing, but felt fine. His mind raced, trying to logically explain what had happened to him. The most straightforward explanation—that he had been reborn—seemed unbelievable. It was the day a grizzly bear attacked him that he finally accepted what was happening to him. He fended off the bear with ease, watching as the wounds the bear had inflicted healed before his eyes.

When Marcus finally made it to Anchorage, he told a miraculous story about surviving the plane crash, not wanting to disrupt his good life. Things were fine for a while, but as the years passed, people noticed that he wasn't aging. So Marcus cashed out of the stock market, faked his own death, and left everything to a new, fake identity that he assumed. He did this again and again through the years, each time growing more frustrated that he couldn't live a normal life. It wasn't until dragons began appearing on Earth that Marcus first transformed into his dragon form—which got the attention of the League of Dragon Walkers. As part of the League, Marcus realized, he could finally be himself and have a real life. With help from the other Dragon Walkers, Marcus got cybernetic implants and a special double-ended Dragon Claw Blade, engineered to amplify his strength while in human form.

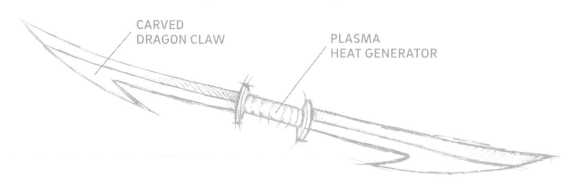

CARVED
DRAGON CLAW

PLASMA
HEAT GENERATOR

▲ DRAGON CLAW BLADE *(above)*

Marcus's double-ended blade is made of actual dragon claws that were discovered on a meteor. Electricity runs through the blades, heating them so they can melt through many kinds of metal.

STATS

- Warrior Class: UEE Covert Guardian
- Physiology: Earth-born human
- Size: 5 ft. to 6 ft. (1.52 to 1.83 m)
- Offensive Capabilities: Survival Blade
- Defensive Capabilities: Moderate armor, Survival Blade

PROFILE

Assigned by a Covert Explorer Captain to watch over and protect secret locations, the Temple Guardian's task is a lonely one. After the Covert Explorer Captain and Warriors find and secure a location, a piece of technology is left there. It's the Temple Guardian's job to stay behind and guard this tech with their life. Typically the hidden location will be an old temple, tomb, or other structure on an uninhabited world or asteroid.

Temple Guardians have a background in archeology and diplomacy, useful in case of encounters with any travelers or explorers. A Guardian must volunteer to be part of the program, but because of the rigorous isolation training, only about one out of every hundred applicants becomes a Temple Guardian. Though the Covert Explorer Captain will relay the coordinates of each hidden location to the UEE, no regular contact is maintained between Temple Guardians and the UEE.

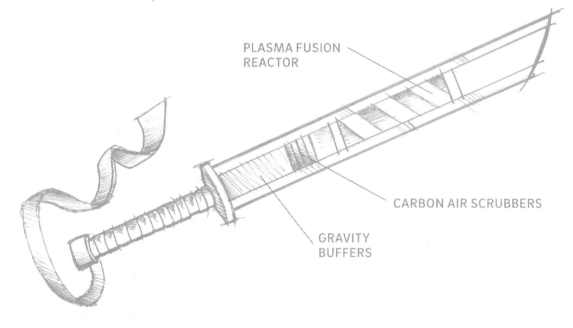

PLASMA FUSION REACTOR

CARBON AIR SCRUBBERS

GRAVITY BUFFERS

▲ SURVIVAL BLADE *(above)*

Temple Guardians are each given a special Survival Blade. It is similar to the Siege Blade, but has added features like gravity buffers built in that allow it to change its weight. By decreasing its weight on the upswing and increasing it on the downswing, the sword is faster and more agile than a Siege Blade, but just as powerful. Fueled by a small plasma fusion reactor, it can generate light and heat, as well as power a concealed carbon scrubber. Many of the hidden structures are unstable, and Guardians sometimes find themselves trapped. If this happens, vents on the sides of the sword filter the air to make it breathable, allowing the Guardian more time to find a way out.

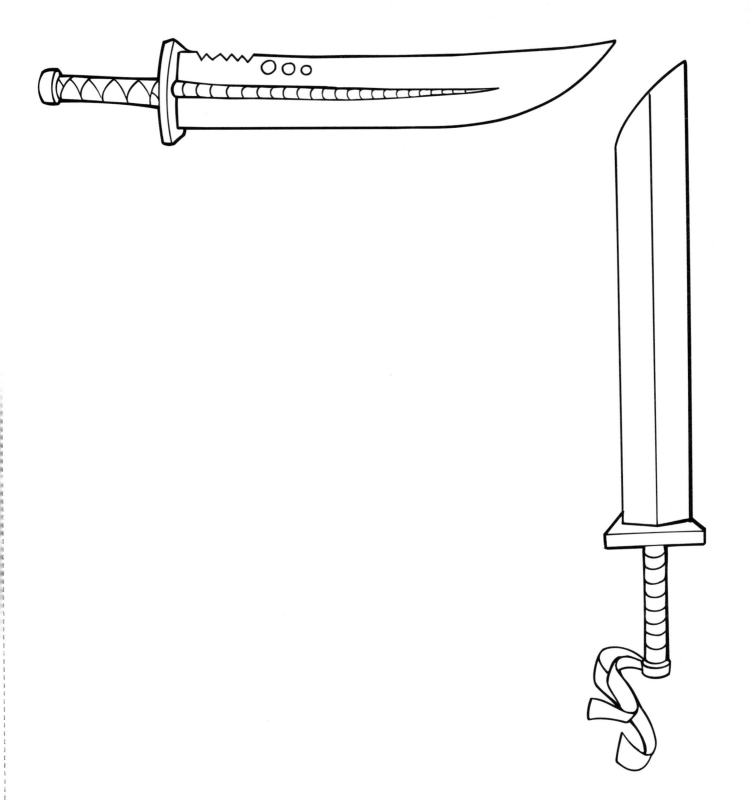

Draw your own original swords and create a profile about each one.

◀ UEE SWORDS *(previous page)*

Now that Earth is a hub for travelers from other worlds, many weapons find their way to Earth. In addition to handheld energy weapons, the UEE collects and develops many traditional weapons, like swords. Though handheld blasters are powerful and diverse, many covert units prefer the quieter, more traditional swords. Swords are also sufficiently bulky to encase upgrades, such as gravity dampeners, to blend tradition with technology. Many swords use technology to amplify abilities warriors have naturally, working in sync with whoever wields the weapon.

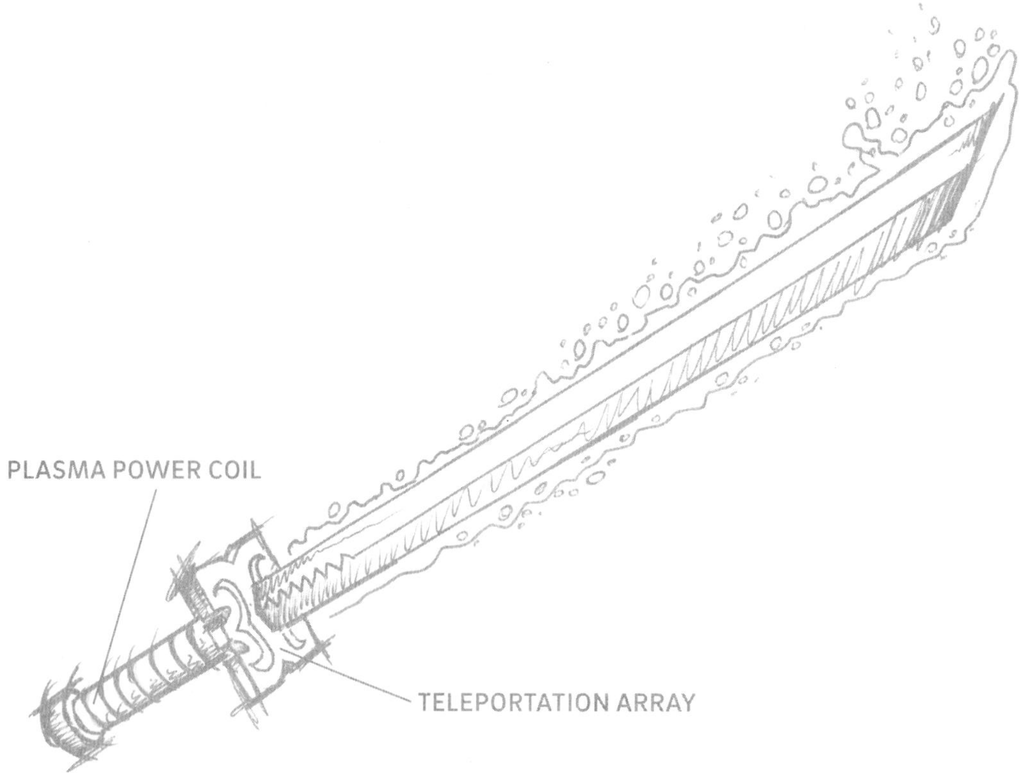

PLASMA POWER COIL
TELEPORTATION ARRAY

▲ PHASE SWORD *(above)*

The UEE gave Claude, the leader of the League of Dragon Walkers, this Phase Sword as a gift in an attempt to build a relationship with him and his organization. The sword's phase shift technology allows anyone using it to teleport short distances as well as pass through solid surfaces like walls. It can also heat up to extreme temperatures, like a Siege Blade can, melting metal objects such as doors and bars.

STATS

- Warrior Class: UEE Covert Ops
- Physiology: Earth-born human
- Size: 5 ft. to 6 ft. (1.52 to 1.83 m)
- Offensive Capabilities: Phase Blade
- Defensive Capabilities: Light armor, Phase Blade cloaking

PROFILE

One of the main missions of the Covert Division of the UEE is to search out hidden locations such as abandoned temples and tombs to scatter and hide Earth's technology. With Earth's technology hidden among the stars, if the planet is ever in grave danger or invaded, humans will still have the resources and power to rebuild. These reconnaissance missions are organized by Covert Explorer Captains. All Captains have a background as UEE pilots and must volunteer for the Explorer training program. Each Captain handpicks their team depending on the area they'll be exploring. They can spend up to a decade studying and researching a location before picking the right Temple Guardian to assign there.

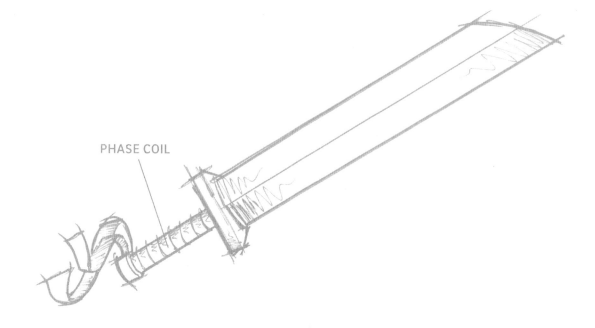

PHASE COIL

▲ **PHASE BLADE** *(above)*

Besides being a powerful blade, Phase Blades can also create a cloaking field, making anything within its field invisible. The cloaking field is delicate, however, so if the user tries to use any other type of disrupting pulse weapon while cloaked, the cloak will disengage. The blade can also be overcharged to allow the user to shift out of phase and pass through solid walls. Unfortunately, this function emits a very high level of radiation that over time hurts the Explorer and can potentially result in the destruction of the blade itself.

STATS

- Warrior Class: Warrior Dragon
- Physiology: Human-born Dragon Walker with cybernetic upgrades

SIZE:

- Human form: 5 ft. 10 in. (1.78 m) tall
- Dragon form: Medium dragon, 24 ft. (7.32 m) long

OFFENSIVE CAPABILITIES:

- Human form: Hand-to-hand combat, Triton Blade
- Dragon form: Claws

DEFENSIVE CAPABILITIES:

- Human form: Heavy armor
- Dragon form: Regenerating Scales

PROFILE

Born in France in the mid-1700s, Claude died during the French Revolution. Shortly after losing his life, he miraculously awoke, disoriented and severely wounded. Though he remembered dying, the memories of his former life were fragments, quickly fading. He watched, transfixed, as the skin around his wounds pulled together and healed. He did not understand it then, but his cells were automatically regenerating. There were other changes he noticed as well: his skin was much tougher; he could tolerate extreme heat; he no longer needed to eat; and his nights were filled with increasingly vivid dreams of fire-breathing monsters. Time passed in the world around him, but Claude did not age. Eventually he settled into dealing antiques—antiques not always procured legally—and became quite wealthy. It was only after the formation of the UEE that he confirmed what he had long believed: there was indeed dragon DNA in his cells.

More than 200 years ago, Claude began to seek others like himself who had the soul of a dragon. Together, they formed a group called the League of Dragon Walkers. All of them had died and regenerated, and many had gained new abilities since being reborn. The strongest Dragon Walkers could even physically transform into dragons. Claude has tirelessly dedicated himself to finding and recruiting Dragon Walkers from around the world and welcoming them into the League.

REGENERATING SCALES

▲ **CLAUDE'S DRAGON FORM** *(above)*

While in dragon form, Claude can communicate telepathically from great distances with other dragon walkers, and even intrude on dreams.

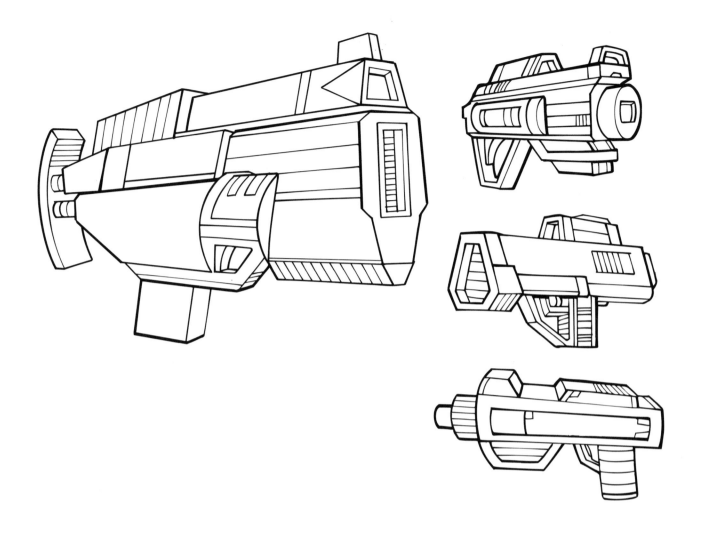

Draw your own original UEE blasters and create a profile about each one.

Thanks to a great deal of research, the UEE has developed the universe's largest array of unique handheld energy weapons. With Earth now a central hub for travelers from other worlds, the UEE developed many weapons based on technology from off-world cultures, including weapons that amplify the user's natural abilities, weapons that manipulate time and space, weapons with targeted teleportation, and cybernetic weapon upgrades for dragons, robots, and humanoids. The UEE researches all the unique powers of these different technologies to incorporate them into their own blasters. Each requires a powerful energy source; some draw their abilities from the user's life force, while others are powered by plasma cells.

QUANTUM COMPRESSED
TITANIUM CASING

QUANTUM
TIME REGULATOR

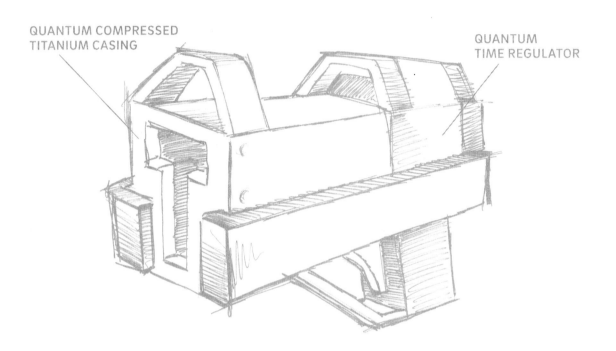

▲ **TRITON BLASTER** (*above*)

The Triton Blaster was the product of years of UEE research. During testing, it proved to be far more powerful than expected. It disrupts the atomic structure of matter, binding and neutralizing all of the atoms in its target, effectively freezing it within its own bubble of time. There is no known way to reverse the effect, so no one knows if whatever is trapped inside the bubble experiences time or not. From the outside, whatever is inside looks like a statue. The blaster's range was highly unpredictable in testing, and in the wrong hands it could be devastating. In theory, if adapted for larger-scale use, it could immobilize a fleet of ships or an entire planet. It was deemed simply too powerful to use. Some fought for it to be destroyed, but in the end it was sent off with the Kagonin Knights for safekeeping in a secret location, in case such a terrible weapon is someday needed.

STATS

- Warrior Class: UEE Specialized Trooper
- Physiology: Earth-born human
- Size: 6 ft. (1.83 m) or taller
- Offensive Capabilities: Multra Blaster
- Defensive Capabilities: Light Alien Arachnid Silk Armor, Shield-Generated Force Field

PROFILE

Special Weapons Attack Officers (SWAOs) are the first unit used for any raids that are not a pitched battle or large-scale offensive. These warriors specialize in subduing threats without killing. They are equipped with light Alien Arachnid Silk Armor as well as a personal shield generator mounted on their back that creates a force field to protect against energy weapon attacks. They also have small plasma cell-powered jets controlled by a neural interface within their suit, allowing them to fly limited distances and hover.

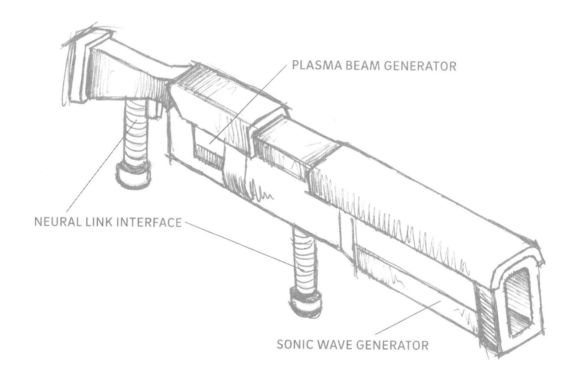

PLASMA BEAM GENERATOR

NEURAL LINK INTERFACE

SONIC WAVE GENERATOR

▲ MULTRA BLASTER *(above)*

Each officer is equipped with a Multipurpose Blaster, also known as a Multra Blaster. This blaster has multiple settings to fire several different types of projectiles, all controlled by a neural interface linked to the officer. It has a wide-beam sonic blast that renders humanoids unconscious within a twenty-foot radius, a sonic blast wave that deactivates small robots, and a lethal plasma beam for use in extreme circumstances. This setting can be quite devastating and works against humans, robots, and heavily armored doors and walls, but depletes the blaster's entire plasma cell power source in only six shots. The Multra Blaster can also be overloaded to self-destruct, which can be useful for destroying a vehicle or small spaceship.

STATS

- Warrior Class: UEE Covert Ops
- Physiology: Earth-born human
- Size: 5 ft. to 6 ft. (1.52 to 1.83 m)
- Offensive Capabilities: Combat Phase Blade
- Defensive Capabilities: Dragon Scale Armor

PROFILE

Typically a small group of four to six Covert Warriors will travel with a Covert Explorer Captain. These soldiers are volunteers and classified as expendable. Their mandate is to sacrifice themselves, if necessary, to maintain the covert status of their mission. A Captain will not think twice about leaving Warriors behind if a mission becomes compromised; Warriors understand this when they volunteer. Leaving Warriors behind can also be a strategic decision to draw attention away from another area. All Forgotten Warriors, as they are called, will maintain loyalty until their death and disavow any association with the UEE if captured. Most Warriors that are left behind simply disappear from sight, blending in somewhere to live out their life on an alien planet, never to be heard from again. No one knows exactly how many Forgotten Warriors have given up their lives for the secrecy of the UEE's covert missions.

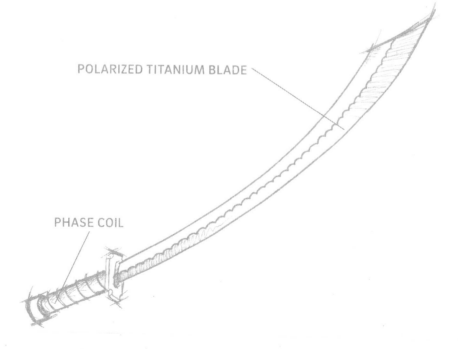

POLARIZED TITANIUM BLADE

PHASE COIL

▲ **COMBAT PHASE BLADE** (above)

Covert Warriors carry a Combat Phase Blade. This Combat version of the Phase Blade is similar to the Captain's Phase Blade, but it is more compact and easier to wield in battle, and its cloaking ability has a smaller protective radius. In addition to the Phase Blades, each Covert Warrior has dragon-scale-enhanced light armor with medical nanobots, similar to the Kagonin Knight's armor, but not as bulky. This armor not only protects the Warriors but also ensures some degree of comfortable survival if they are ever left behind without resources.

STATS

- Warrior Class: UEE Sword Master
- Physiology: Earth-born human
- Size: 5 ft. to 6 ft. (1.52 to 1.83 m)
- Offensive Capabilities: Sword fighting
- Defensive Capabilities: Light armor

PROFILE

There is a large division of the UEE that is devoted to sword fighting and hand-to-hand combat training, and it is run by Kente, the Strategic Commander of the UEE. Kente created an elite class of instructors that he trains personally, called Sword Masters. In addition to mastering hand-to-hand combat, Sword Masters are responsible for knowing how to use all UEE swords in the most optimal way. In order for Sword Masters to complete their training, they must have been deployed in at least three real combat situations and shown exemplary performance on the battlefield. Once a Sword Master passes this test, they are then certified to instruct all other UEE forces in hand-to-hand combat. Though many enter the program, most do not make it through; currently, there are only 20 certified Sword Masters in the UEE.

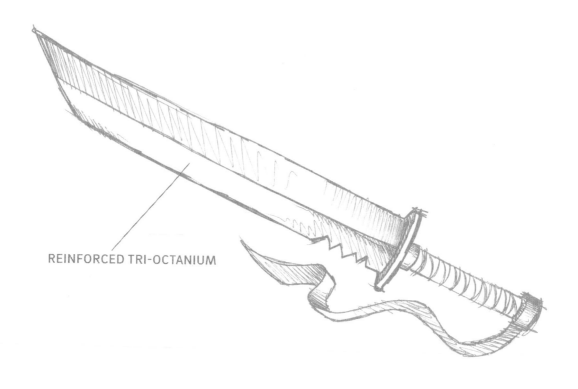

REINFORCED TRI-OCTANIUM

▲ CEREMONIAL SWORD *(above)*

After Sword Masters complete their training, Kente presents them with a unique technology-free ceremonial sword that he has hand crafted. Each sword is made of a rare alloy of various metals, found on meteors, that is called Tri-Octanium. It's the only type of metal that can cut through polarized titanium with ease.

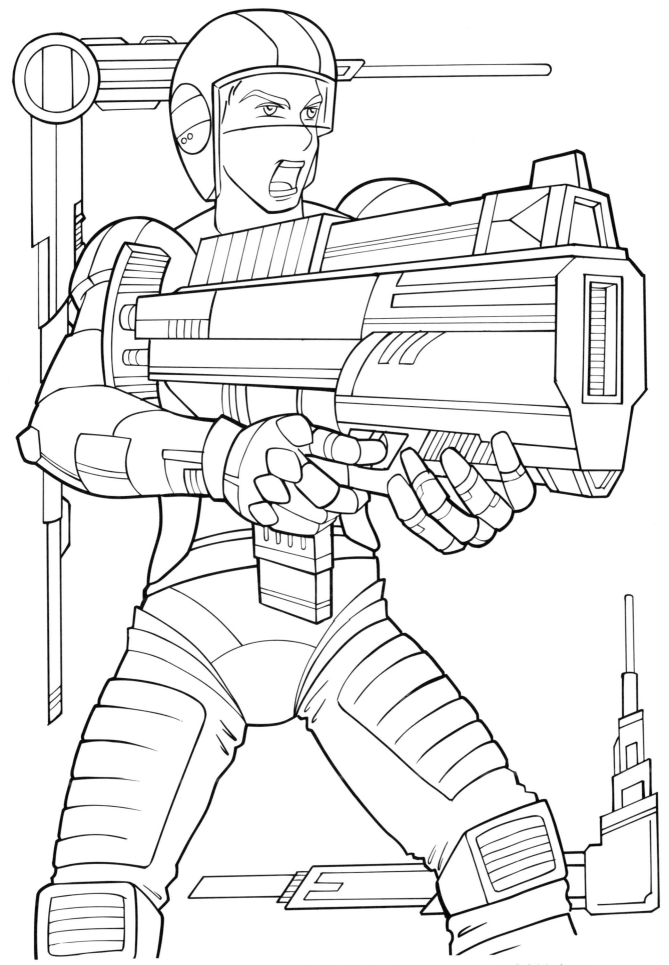

STATS

- Warrior Class: UEE Trooper
- Physiology: Earth-born human
- Size: 5 ft. to 6 ft. (1.52 to 1.83 m)
- Offensive Capabilities: Pulse Rifle
- Defensive Capabilities: Moderate armor

PROFILE

All able-bodied Earth citizens are encouraged to serve at least two years in the UEE's armed forces, and those who do are highly respected. This is partly to ensure that all citizens know how to defend Earth in the event of a planetary invasion. The service is not mandatory but is seen as a very honorable choice that reflects well on the volunteer's family and social status. The UEE Trooper is the most common form of service, designed for those who want to volunteer to contribute to Earth's protection but don't necessarily have a specialized skill set. There are so many Troopers that all other units of the UEE combined would only amount to a fraction of the total Trooper count. Recognized as a sort of general police force of Earth, Troopers help with supply lines, provide security, enforce laws, patrol spaceports, and perform inspections of ships in spaceports. They maintain peace and have special training in alien languages and nonlethal crowd control, but are always on call in case of a large-scale battle.

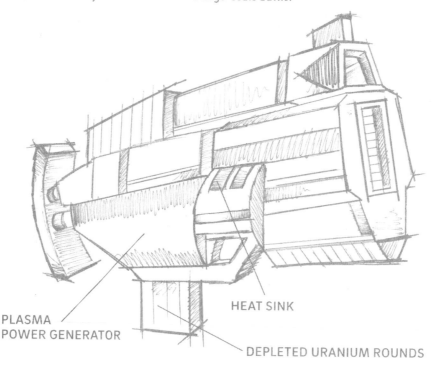

PLASMA
POWER GENERATOR

HEAT SINK

DEPLETED URANIUM ROUNDS

▲ PULSE RIFLE (above)

Every trooper receives a basic Pulse Rifle on their first day of training. The Pulse Rifle is the most common weapon in the UEE. It uses a depleted uranium round propelled at a high velocity by a small amount of ignited plasma. Every single warrior of the UEE, even the more specialized units, is trained in the use of this standard weapon.

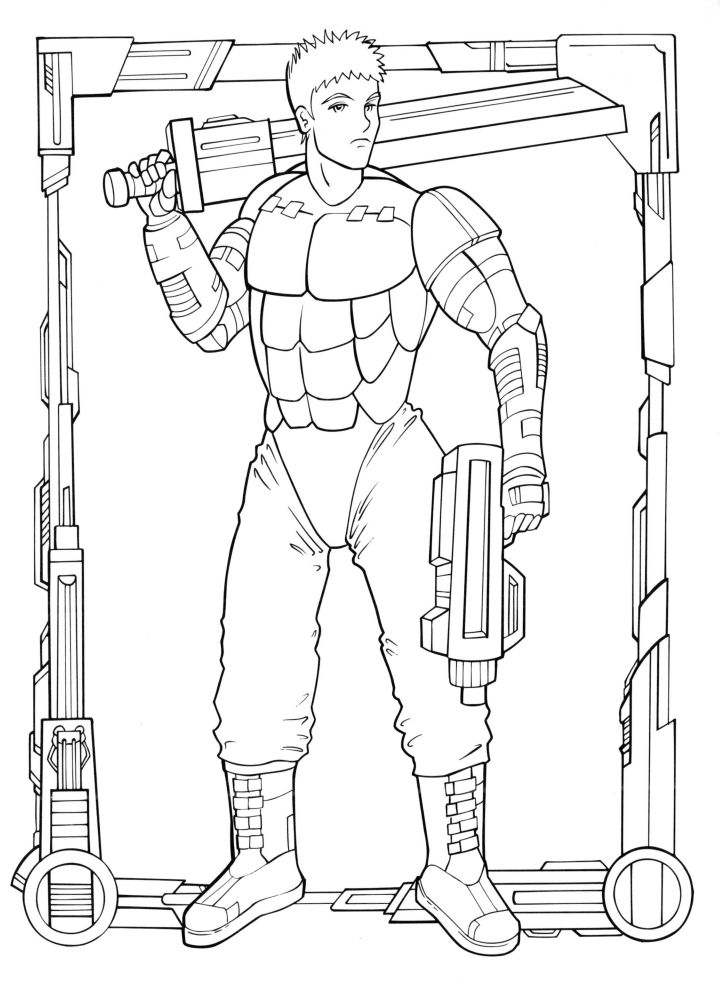

STATS

- Warrior Class: UEE Trooper
- Physiology: Earth-born human
- Size: 5 ft. to 6 ft. (1.52 to 1.83 m)
- Offensive Capabilities: Silence Pulse Pistol
- Defensive Capabilities: Light armor

PROFILE

UEE Field Scouts are a voluntary, common unit designed mainly for reconnaissance and intelligence gathering. There is a Field Scout platoon in each battalion. Scouts do battlefield recon about troop movement and numbers, sabotage such as setting traps, and survey land ahead of troops. Field Scouts are lightly armored and tend to avoid conflict, entering battle only when absolutely necessary.

PULSE SILENCER

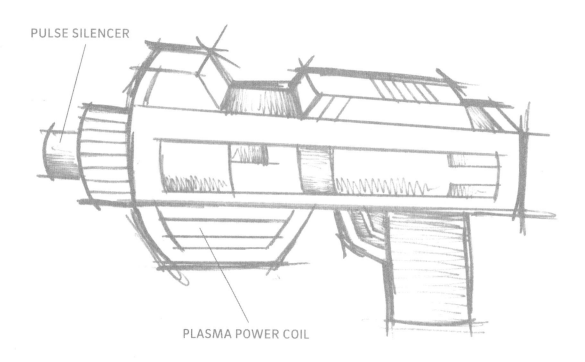

PLASMA POWER COIL

▲ SILENCE PULSE PISTOL *(above)*

Field Scouts are equipped with a Silence Pulse Pistol for self-defense. It makes absolutely no noise but has a limited range. In addition to the Silence Pulse Pistol, Field Scouts tend to also use a sword, such as a reduced-size Siege Blade, to help break down doors, cut through brush, or clear any other obstruction they might encounter.

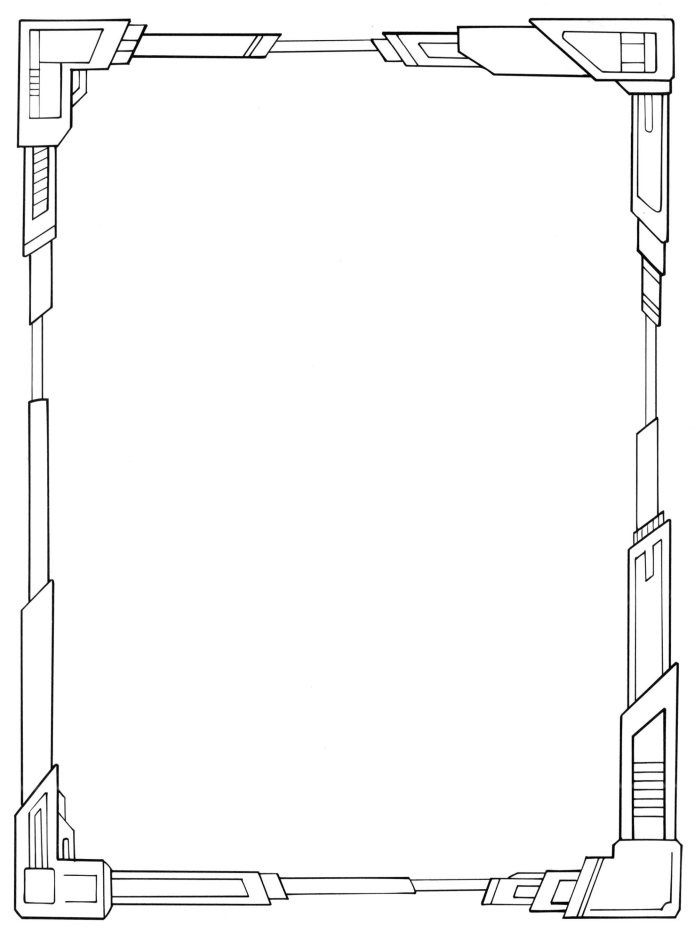

Draw your own Warrior and use the back of the page to create a profile.

STATS

- Warrior Class: _____
- Physiology: _____
- Size: _____
- Offensive Capabilities: _____
- Defensive Capabilities: _____

PROFILE